For all those who love, and fight for, the treasures of biodiversity – N.D.
For Maisie, Georgia and Felix – L.S.

STERLING CHILDREN'S BOOKS
New York

An Imprint of Sterling Publishing Co., Inc.
1166 Avenue of the Americas
New York, NY 10036

First Sterling edition published in 2018.

ISBN 978-1-4549-3188-1

Distributed in Canada by Sterling Publishing
c/o Canadian Manda Group, 664 Annette Street
Toronto, Ontario M6S 2C8, Canada

For information about custom editions, special sales, and premium and corporate purchases,
please contact Sterling Special Sales at 800-805-5489 or specialsales@sterlingpublishing.com.

Manufactured in China
Lot #:
2 4 6 8 10 9 7 5 3 1
05/18

sterlingpublishing.com

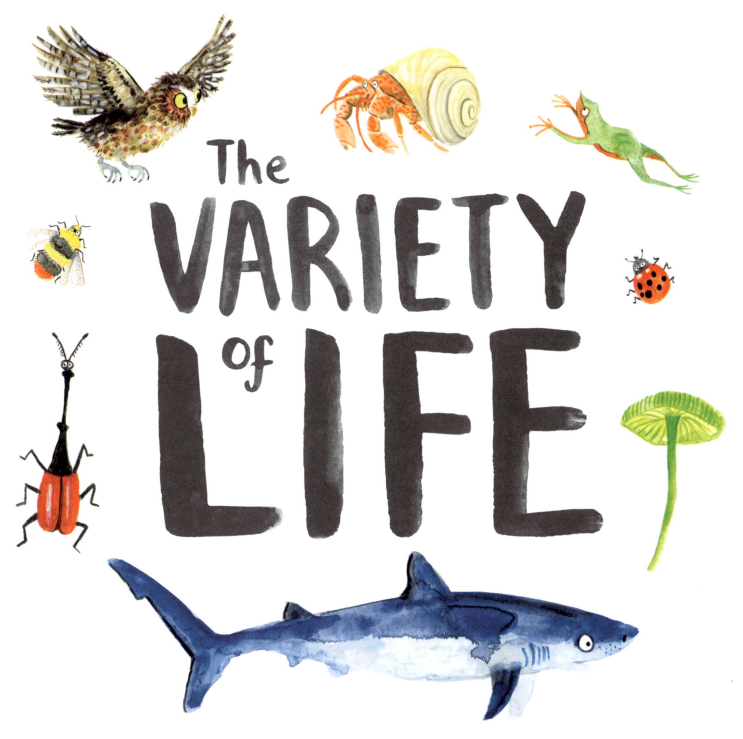

The VARIETY of LIFE

Written by
Nicola Davies

Illustrated by
Lorna Scobie

STERLING CHILDREN'S BOOKS
New York

OUR PLANET IS FULL OF LIFE!

There are living things everywhere, from high mountains to deep oceans, from burning deserts to icy poles. To be able to survive in such different places plants and animals need different bodies and different abilities. That's why there are many kinds of living things, each one suited to a particular place.

Scientists call a *kind* of living thing a *species*. So far they have found and named almost two million species but there could be many more that haven't yet been named, possibly as many as ten million! Together, this amazing variety of species has a scientific name, too: it's called biodiversity, and it's a precious treasure.

But human beings are cutting down forests, polluting oceans, and changing the climate, making it harder and harder for many species to survive. Any species whose numbers fall year after year is in danger of being lost from the world; it is threatened with extinction. Extinction means that all the members of that species are dead; the species is gone forever.

The first thing that we can do to try and stop this from happening and keep that precious biodiversity safe, is to notice and name as many living things as we can. If a species has no name, it can be lost without us even realizing.

Some of the names for animals and plants are words that we all know well—whale, butterfly, frog, mushroom . . . But if we only ever use those words, then we might never notice that there are many different species of whales, butterflies, frogs, and mushrooms!

This book is all about noticing how many different species there are. By the time you have finished reading it, you will know the names of many of them. You will be able to hold a little piece of the treasure of biodiversity in your heart and help to stop it from slipping away, unknown and unnamed.

A NOTE ABOUT ANIMAL NAMES

Every kind of living thing or species has a scientific name which is in two parts like this: *Ursus arctos*

The first part tells you what the species is related to, sort of like its last name—in this case, "bear"—and the second part shows which member of the family it is—in this case, "brown." No two living things have the same two-part name, so *Ursus arctos* can only mean one species, the brown bear.

You'll find these scientific names written after every English name in this book; sometimes there will *only* be a scientific name as the species hasn't been given a "common" name.

A NOTE ABOUT EXTINCTION

When you are reading this book you will come across a few species marked with a ★. This means these species are threatened with extinction.

BEAR

Bears may look cute, but they are not cuddly teddies; they have strong jaws, feet with long claws, and they are very strong. All eight species of bear can stand easily on their back legs; even the smallest, the sun bear, is as tall as a man, and the largest, the polar bear, stands almost ten feet high. Bears can eat many different things: leaves, fruit, insects, fish, birds, or other mammals, but some concentrate on just one food type.

BROWN (GRIZZLY) BEAR
(Ursus arctos)

SPECTACLED BEAR ★
(Tremarctos ornatus)
This species lives in the forests and grasslands of the Andes and eats all kinds of plants.

GIANT PANDA ★
(Ailuropoda melanoleuca)
This distinctive bear feeds mainly on bamboo and spends up to fourteen hours a day eating to get the nutrients that it needs.

SUN BEAR ★
(Helarctos malayanus)

The small sun bear spends a lot of time in the trees, eating fruit and making treetop nests to sleep in at night.

This large bear eats anything from moths to salmon, berries to deer, and lives in many habitats across Europe, Asia, and North America.

8 SPECIES

SLOTH BEAR ★
(Melursus ursinus)
This Asian bear has long claws for digging and uses its mouth like a vacuum cleaner to suck up ants and termites.

ASIAN BLACK BEAR ★
(Ursus thibetanus)
This medium-size bear from the mountain forests of South Asia is a good climber that eats a wide range of plant and animal foods.

AMERICAN BLACK BEAR
(Ursus americanus)
There are more black bears in existence than all the other species put together. They are found throughout North America.

POLAR BEAR ★
(Ursus maritimus)
It hunts seals on the frozen Arctic ocean and goes hungry when the ice melts.

The blue whale is an ocean giant, the most enormous creature ever to have lived on earth. Most of the largest species of whale sieve tiny food (like krill) from the ocean using baleen plates not teeth. These are called baleen whales. Others are hunters with mouths full of pointed teeth and are known as the toothed whales. That group includes sperm and killer whales and dolphins—on the next page!

BLUE WHALE (Balaenoptera musculus) ★ This immense whale is over twice as heavy as the biggest dinosaur.

KILLER WHALE
(Orcinus orca)

Also called "orcas," these whales hunt in groups to catch fish, seals, and even other whales.

PYGMY RIGHT WHALE (Caperea marginata)
These are the smallest baleen whales, but they are still elephant-size.

85 SPECIES

BOWHEAD WHALE (Balaena mysticetus)
Lives on the edge of the Arctic ice and eats tiny shrimp-like creatures called krill.

HUMPBACK WHALE (Megaptera novaeangliae)
This species uses nets of bubbles to help catch shoals of fish and krill.

SPERM WHALE ★ (Physeter macrocephalus)
Sperm whales hunt squid in water over 6,000 feet deep, using sonar to find their prey.

DOLPHIN

BOTTLENOSE DOLPHIN (Tursiops truncatus)

The bottlenose is the most familiar dolphin, found in warmer waters close to land worldwide.

MAUI'S DOLPHIN ★ (Cephalorhynchus hectori maui)

The smallest and rarest dolphin, also known as popoto. Fewer than 70 survive in the wild.

PINK RIVER DOLPHIN ★ (Inia geoffrensis)

Also called the boto or Amazon river dolphin, it has tiny eyes, as the waters of the Amazon are too murky to see through.

Short Beaked COMMON DOLPHIN (Delphinus delphis)

This species features in 3,500-year-old mosaics on the Greek island of Crete.

43 SPECIES

SOUTHERN RIGHT WHALE DOLPHIN (Lissodelphis peronii)

These are found in the cold waters around Antarctica.

RISSO'S DOLPHIN (Grampus griseus)

White scars crisscross the gray body of this distinctive creature, also known as grampus.

SPINNER DOLPHIN (Stenella longirostris)

The spinner is found spinning and somersaulting in tropical seas in super pods of several thousand creatures.

COMMERSON'S DOLPHIN (Cephalorhynchus commersonii)

Found only around Tierra Del Fuego in South America, the Falkland Islands, and the Kerguelen Islands.

All dolphins are fast-swimming hunters. They don't really smile; it's just the way their jaws are shaped, with up to 250 teeth for grabbing slippery fish and squid! Most species live in the ocean, but a few live in rivers. All have a rounded forehead (called a melon) which contains their sonar system: they use the echoes of their own voices to find prey. Dolphins almost always live in groups, called pods, that travel, and often hunt, together.

SHEEP

MOUFLON ★ (Ovis orientalis)
Found across Europe and Asia. Some mountains and islands have their own varieties, which are threatened with extinction, such as Cyprian wild sheep.

THINHORN OR DALL'S SHEEP (Ovis dalli)
Beautiful white sheep from the highest, coldest mountains in the far northwest of North America.

AMERICAN BIGHORN SHEEP (Ovis canadensis)
Big tough sheep from mountains and deserts of western North America. Males have huge curved horns for fighting.

BLUE SHEEP ★ (Pseudois nayaur)
Its blue-gray coat blends with the snow and rock of the Himalayas. Both males and females have horns!

Humans have been keeping sheep for wool, meat, and milk for at least 9,000 years. There are more than 200 breeds of domestic sheep, but they all belong to one species, descended from the wild mouflon, from the deserts and mountains of Europe and Asia. Unlike them, wild sheep are fast and feisty; most have horns, which are larger on the males or rams, and used in fierce fights over the females or ewes.

6 SPECIES

SNOW SHEEP (Ovis nivicola)
The Russian version of American bighorn from the mountains of Siberia.

ARGALI (Ovis ammon)
The biggest wild sheep. Found in mountains of central Asia. A male's horns can weigh up to 48 pounds!

BARBADOS BLACKBELLY (Ovis aries)
Bred in the Caribbean from domestic sheep brought from Africa.

LACAUNE SHEEP (Ovis aries)
Bred in France for milk production. Sheep's milk can be good for people who are intolerant of cow's milk.

MERINO SHEEP (Ovis aries)
First bred in Spain for their thick wool, they are now the most common sheep in Australia.

MONKEY

RHESUS MACAQUE
(Macaca mulatta)
This species is commonly found in Indian cities, living on rooftops, climbing power cables, and raiding trash cans.

ANGOLAN BLACK-AND-WHITE COLOBUS MONKEY
(Colobus angolensis)
This African species has stumps for thumbs so there is less chance of it getting injured as it jumps around the treetops.

GOLDEN SNUB-NOSED MONKEY ★ (Rhinopithecus roxellana)
These lovely creatures live only in the mountain forests of central China, which are being cut down, putting them in danger.

BROWN CAPUCHIN MONKEY
(Sapajus apella)
These small, clever, tool-using monkeys live in the Amazon forests.

Monkeys are like us. They do things like we do: cuddle their babies, play, and squabble. Unlike humans and chimps (which are not monkeys, but apes, and are our closest animal relatives), monkeys are not hunters, but rather, eat leaves, fruit, and nuts. They are excellent climbers, and some even have tails they can use like an extra hand. Most live in forests, and many are threatened by habitat destruction.

260 SPECIES

BLACK-HANDED SPIDER MONKEY ★
(Ateles geoffroyi)
Also known as Geoffroy's
spider monkey, this species
lives high in the rainforest
in Central America and can
use its tail as a fifth limb.

DIANA MONKEY ★ (Cercopithecus diana)
These agile monkeys live high in the West African
rainforest and almost never come down to the ground.

PATAS MONKEY (Erythrocebus patas)
Living on the grasslands of Africa, Patas monkeys
run rather than climb to avoid danger.

PROBOSCIS MONKEY ★ (Nasalis larvatus)
These endangered monkeys living in the forests
of Borneo have a big belly for digesting leaves.
Males have big noses for showing off to females!

BAT

GREATER HORSESHOE BAT
(*Rhinolophus ferrumequinum*)
Super agile flight allows these European bats to catch beetles and moths in midair.

KITTI'S HOGNOSED BAT ★
(*Craseonycteris thonglongyai*)

Also known as the bumblebee bat, this is the tiniest of all bats (and mammals) and flies between the leaves in forests of Myanmar and Thailand to catch insects.

INDIAN FLYING FOX (*Pteropus giganteus*)

The flying fox has a six-foot wingspan for long-distance flying to find fruit.

GREATER FALSE VAMPIRE BAT
(*Megaderma lyra*)

A hunter of mice, reptiles, and other bats, this species is found across much of Asia.

1,240 SPECIES

A dark shape fluttering in the nighttime sky is all we usually see. But up close, bats are fascinating. Their wings are made of fine skin stretched between finger bones, and their bodies are covered in fine fur. As they fly, bats make high-pitched squeaks that our ears can't hear, and the echoes give them a detailed picture in sound, so they can find food in total darkness. Flight and echolocation together have allowed bats to find many ways to make a living in the nighttime world.

HONDURAN WHITE BAT ★ (Ectophylla alba)
This small bat sleeps by day in tents made by biting into the middle of rainforest leaves.

FISHERMAN BAT (Noctilio leporinus)
Also known as the greater bulldog bat, this large species uses sonar to spot the ripples in a pond, then hooks out the fish using its huge feet.

COMMON VAMPIRE BAT (Desmodus rotundus)
This mouse-size South American bat feeds on blood, preferring animal to human blood.

MEXICAN LONG-NOSED BAT ★ (Leptonycteris nivalis)
As they feed on nectar of the blue agave, these bats carry pollen from flower to flower, pollinating them and allowing the plant to make seeds.

HAMMERHEAD FRUIT BAT (Hypsignathus monstrosus)
The honking mating calls of the hammerhead males ring out from riverside trees in Central Africa.

MOUSE

Mice can live in tiny spaces, eat anything, and have a lot of babies, and that's made them a big success. House mice live wherever there are humans, but there are mice that live in almost every habitat on earth: mice with long tails for balancing that live in trees, mice with long claws for digging and burrowing. Most mice eat seeds or insects, but there are some that eat fish, and even other mice!

HOUSE MOUSE (Mus musculus)
One pair of house mice can have thousands of descendants in a year.

LONG-CLAWED MOLE MOUSE (Geoxus valdivianus)
This mouse burrows in forests and grasslands on the southern tip of South America.

YELLOW-NECKED WOOD MOUSE (Apodemus flavicollis)
These seed-eating mice from European woodlands are expert climbers.

DARWIN'S LEAF-EARED MOUSE (Phyllotis darwini)
This species lives in the cold, dry Atacama desert in Chile.

NORTHERN GRASSHOPPER MOUSE (Onychomys leucogaster)
Also known as the killer mouse, this species lives in the western USA and Canada and eats insects, lizards, and other mice.

1,000+ SPECIES

CHIBCHAN WATER MOUSE
(Chibchanomys trichotis)

Feeding on snails and small fish, this species lives along streams in the Andes mountains in South America.

HARVEST MOUSE (Micromys minutus)
These tiny mice weigh the same as a teaspoon of sugar and nest in the tops of grass and corn.

COTTON MOUSE (Peromyscus gossypinus)
Found in southeastern USA and Canada, the favorite home of this species is the underground burrows made by tortoises.

FOUR-STRIPED MOUSE (Rhabdomys pumilio)
Found all over southern Africa, the whole family helps to rear new babies.

MASTIFF (Canis familiaris)
One of the oldest breeds, known since Roman times, bred for guarding.

MEXICAN HAIRLESS (Canis familiaris)
Bred 3,000 years ago by the Aztecs, the Mexican hairless, or "Xoloitzcuintli," were originally intended to be a living hot-water bottle.

SPANIEL (Canis familiaris)
These lively dogs were bred to scare birds and animals out of bushes so they could be shot, then retrieved by the dog.

BORDER COLLIE (Canis familiaris)
Wolves and other wild dogs herd their prey. Sheepdogs are bred to herd without killing.

Around 30,000 years ago humans began to use wolves to help them hunt. Over time, the wolves that lived with humans changed into a new species, the domestic dog. Humans bred different kinds to do different jobs, so today there are hundreds of dog breeds. Domestic dogs are not the same species as true wild dogs that have never been tamed by humans.

DACHSHUND (Canis familiaris)
These small dogs have short legs and a long body, bred to chase rabbits out of their holes.

SALUKI (Canis familiaris)
Slender and fast, these dogs were bred in the Middle East around 3,000 years ago for hunting in the desert.

BUSH DOG ★ (Speothos venaticus)
These dogs are hardy and fierce pack hunters that kill tapirs, agoutis, and pacas in the forests and grasslands of South America.

AFRICAN WILD DOG ★ (Lycaon pictus)
This is an efficient pack hunter from southern Africa that can run for hours without stopping.

PARROT

SWIFT PARROT ★ (*Lathamus discolor*)

These brightly colored parrots feed on gum-tree nectar and nest in treeholes in Southern Australia.

AFRICAN GREY PARROT ★ (*Psittacus erithacus*)

The most popular pet because of their ability to copy human voices and "talk." There are far more of this species in cages than in the wild.

HYACINTH MACAW ★ (*Anodorhynchus hyacinthinus*)

Macaws are big parrots from the Amazon, and hyacinth macaws are the biggest species of all. They are often taken from the wild to be pets.

It's easy to spot a parrot with its curved beak and bright feathers. Their beak is an all-round tool kit, which they use, together with their clinging feet, to do all sorts of jobs from tree climbing to nut cracking. But their bright feathers have meant that too many have been taken from the wild as pets. Also, many parrot species are found in tropical forests and are threatened by habitat destruction.

356
SPECIES

KEA (Nestor notabilis) ★

Known as the "mountain clown" in New Zealand, this clever parrot loves to play tricks like stealing ski gloves.

BLUE-CROWNED HANGING PARROT (loriculus galgulus)

Found in the forests of Borneo and Malaysia, this small parrot sleeps hanging upside down, like a bat!

SAINT VINCENT PARROT ★ (Amazona guildingii)

This large parrot lives only on the tiny island of Saint Vincent in the Caribbean.

OWL PARROT ★ (Strigops habroptilus)

Heavy as a domestic cat, this flightless parrot from New Zealand, also known as the kakapo, is very rare: fewer than 200 survive in the wild.

BUFF-FACED PYGMY PARROT (Micropsitta pusio)

Light as a pack of gum, this is the world's smallest parrot and lives in Papua New Guinea, eating lichens, fungi, and insects.

OWL

EURASIAN EAGLE OWL (Bubo bubo)

With a wingspan bigger than a tall man, eagle owls have the strength and power to carry off a deer fawn.

ELF OWL (Micrathene whitneyi)
Small enough to fit in a teacup, this North American owl hunts insects and scorpions, and nests in desert cacti.

BARN OWL (Tyto alba)
The most widespread species of owl, and also one of the most widespread of all birds, living in Europe, America, Africa, India, and Australia.

Owls may look cute but they are expert nighttime hunters. They have huge eyes to see in the faintest light, so big that they can't move them and have to turn their head for all-around viewing. Their saucer-shaped faces gather sounds into their sensitive ears, which are hidden under the feathers (and not the feathery tufts that some owls display). They swoop down on silent wings to stab their victims with needle-sharp claws.

216 SPECIES

TAWNY OWL (Strix aluco)
The tawny owl's "twit-twoo" call is familiar in parks and gardens across Europe, and is even mentioned in Shakespeare's plays.

SNOWY OWL (Bubo scandiacus)
These Arctic owls must hunt by day in the summer when there are 24 hours of daylight.

SOKOKE SCOPS OWL ★ (Otus ireneae)
This small owl hunts insects, reptiles, and small mammals in East Africa. Its numbers are dropping as its favorite forests are being cut down.

BLAKISTON'S FISH OWL ★ (Bubo blakistoni)
This large owl is the size of a one-year-old human and snatches salmon from rivers in China and Japan.

SPECTACLED OWL (Pulsatrix perspicillata)
This species hunts in the rainforests of South America.

DUCK

Ducks live on ponds, lakes, streams, rivers, and the sea and are shaped for life in their watery worlds with webbed feet for paddling and waterproof feathers. Most eat tiny creatures living in or on the water, or water plants but a few catch fish. Male ducks, known as drakes, have bright feathers to show off to the females, whose dull brown feathers keep them hidden while they care for their eggs and ducklings.

MALLARD (Anas platyrhynchos)
The most widespread duck species, found all across the world in wild places and parks.

SHOVELER DUCK (Anas clypeata)
This duck's huge, scoop-shaped beak helps it to skim food from the water surface.

COMMON GOLDENEYE (Bucephala clangula)
The drake goldeneye show off to their females with a fast head flick and a ringing cry.

MERGANSER (Mergus merganser)
A thin beak with a spiky edge helps this duck catch slippery fish.

134 SPECIES

KING EIDER DUCK
(Somateria spectabilis)
This large sea duck dives
to find shellfish that it crushes
with its wedge-shaped beak.

MANDARIN DUCK
(Aix galericulata)
Lives on woodland streams and lakes and nests in
tree holes so the ducklings have to jump to reach the ground.

PINTAIL (Anas acuta)
The pintail's long neck means it can
reach underwater food that other
ducks, like mallards, can't get to.

Female

TORRENT DUCK
(Merganetta armata)
A slim body and strong
legs help this duck swim in
fast-flowing mountain rivers.

PENGUIN

EMPEROR PENGUIN
(Aptenodytes forsteri)

World's deepest diving bird, famous for breeding in the heart of winter.

LITTLE BLUE PENGUIN (Eudyptula minor)

Smaller than a milk carton, these penguins live in New Zealand and Southern Australia.

MACARONI PENGUIN ★
(Eudyptes chrysolophus)

This is the most numerous penguin, but its numbers are falling fast.

17 SPECIES

The Antarctic is a tough place to survive, but as there are no predators on the land, penguins don't need to be able to fly when they come ashore. Their wings are narrow, rubbery flippers, their feet are paddles, and their feathers make an insulated drysuit so they can swim and dive to catch krill, fish, and squid. Penguins like company and nest in huge colonies of tens of thousands of birds.

GALAPAGOS PENGUIN ★ (Spheniscus mendiculus)

The most northerly penguin.
It lives in the cold current
around the Galapagos islands.

CHINSTRAP PENGUIN (Pygoscelis antarcticus)

Like all penguins, chinstraps form a strong pair bond
and work together to raise their young.

ADÉLIE PENGUIN
(Pygoscelis adeliae)

KING PENGUIN
(Aptenodytes patagonicus)

Black-and-white coats make penguins
hard for predators to spot underwater.

These penguins dive almost as deep
as emperors but like to breed in summer!

SNAKE

Snakes' tube-like bodies can move over any sort of ground, allowing them to climb, burrow, and even swim, so they can survive in different habitats. All snakes are hunters; some (the constrictors) use their long bodies to suffocate their prey, while others kill with a venomous bite. They have poor sight and don't have ears, but can feel sound as vibration through their bodies. Smell is their most important sense, and their constantly flicking tongue samples scents from the air.

YELLOW-BELLIED SEA SNAKE

(Pelamis platura)

VARIABLE CORAL SNAKE (Micrurus diastema)

Most snakes are camouflaged, but this small snake's bright colors warn that it's very venomous.

This snake lives in tropical oceans, ambushing fish and killing them with its highly toxic venom.

EUROPEAN ADDER (Vipera berus)

INDIAN COBRA
(Naja naja)

This big hunter from India tracks its prey and kills it with a venomous bite.

Most snakes live where it's always warm, but adders survive cold winters by hibernating.

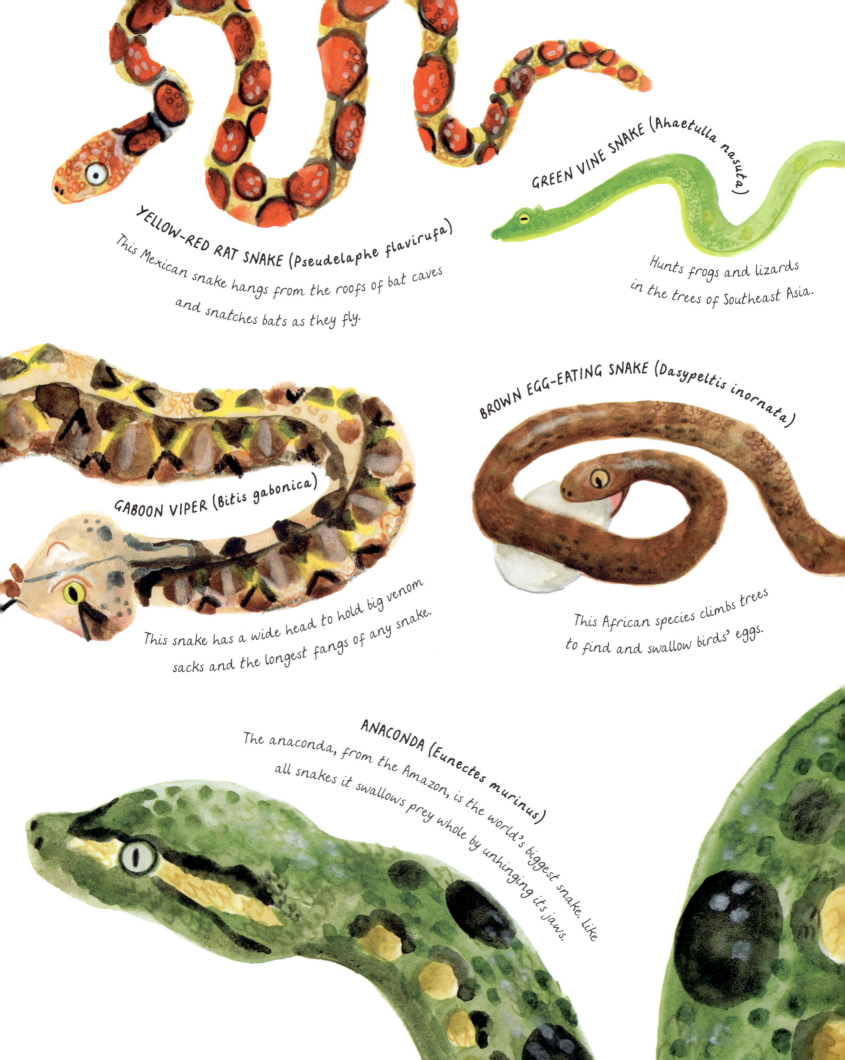

YELLOW-RED RAT SNAKE (Pseudelaphe flavirufa)

This Mexican snake hangs from the roofs of bat caves and snatches bats as they fly.

GREEN VINE SNAKE (Ahaetulla nasuta)

Hunts frogs and lizards in the trees of Southeast Asia.

GABOON VIPER (Bitis gabonica)

This snake has a wide head to hold big venom sacks and the longest fangs of any snake.

BROWN EGG-EATING SNAKE (Dasypeltis inornata)

This African species climbs trees to find and swallow birds' eggs.

ANACONDA (Eunectes murinus)

The anaconda, from the Amazon, is the world's biggest snake. Like all snakes it swallows prey whole by unhinging its jaws.

LIZARD

GREEN ANOLE LIZARD (Anolis carolinensis)

Runs up trees using sticky toes for grip.
Males have a red throat flap to warn
other males off their patch!

SULAWESI LINED GLIDING LIZARD (Draco spilonotus)
Skin flaps on the side of this lizard's slender
body let it glide from tree to tree.

**VIVIPAROUS LIZARD
(Zootoca vivipara)**

This little lizard lives on heaths in
southern England and gives birth to live young,
unlike most lizards, which lay eggs.

**ROUNDTAIL HORNED LIZARD
(Phrynosoma modestum)**

This desert-dwelling lizard has spiny
scales and squirts blood from its eyes
to keep predators like coyotes away.

COMMON WALL LIZARD (Podarcis muralis)

Like most lizards this one can escape by leaving its
tail behind in the predator's mouth if attacked.

**6,000
SPECIES**

Lizards have thick, scaly skin that stops them from drying out, and eggs that are tough and leathery, so they can survive in some of the driest places on Earth. Nearly all lizards are predators. Most run or climb to find food but some are burrowers and have short legs for digging, or no legs at all. Lizards often signal to each other using brightly colored patches or flaps of skin.

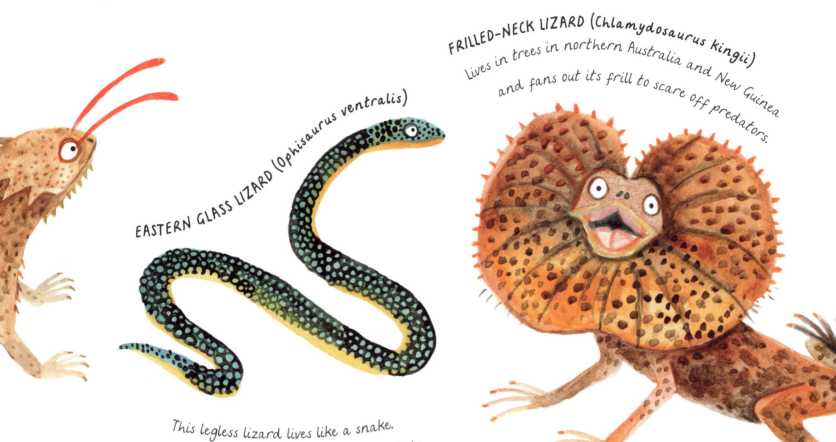

FRILLED-NECK LIZARD (Chlamydosaurus kingii)
Lives in trees in northern Australia and New Guinea and fans out its frill to scare off predators.

EASTERN GLASS LIZARD (Ophisaurus ventralis)

This legless lizard lives like a snake.
But unlike snakes, legless lizards have eyelids.

ASIAN WATER MONITOR LIZARD (Varanus salvator)

Can run fast and swim long distances and will eat anything alive or dead, including other monitor lizards.

FROG

Frogs need water; their thin skin dries out easily, and their eggs and tadpoles need to be wet to turn into frogs. But they have found ways to survive in most habitats, especially rainforests which can be full of their mating calls at night. When habitats are disturbed, frogs are often the first to suffer and many species are now threatened.

NORTHERN GLASS FROG
(Centrolenella fleischmanni)

These almost see-through frogs lay eggs on leaves and the tadpoles drop to the water below.

RED-EYED TREE FROG
(Agalychnis callidryas)

These frogs are camouflaged against the bright green leaves of the rainforest—but their large red eyes scare predators.

EUROPEAN COMMON FROG
(Rana temporaria)

This widespread species hibernates all winter and comes out in the spring to visit ponds and lay eggs in the water.

ARGENTINE ORNATE HORNED FROG
(Ceratophrys ornata)

This large frog from the grasslands of South America will eat anything that it can get into its wide mouth.

4,800 SPECIES

PURPLE FROG ★ (Nasikabatrachus sahyadrensis)

Avoids the Indian dry season by burying itself underground.
It comes out for a few weeks in the rainy season to lay eggs.

FLAMING POISON-ARROW FROG (Oophaga pumilio)

The females of this small South American frog carry
their tadpoles to rain pools in the tops of trees.

DARWIN'S FROG ★
(Rhinoderma darwinii)

Males swallow the female's eggs
and keep them wet in their throats until
they turn into froglets that males "throw up."

WORLD'S SMALLEST FROG
(Paedophryne amauensis)

This minute species
(just 0.27 inches in length)
was discovered in New Guinea in 2012.

WALLACE'S FLYING FROG
(Rhacophorus nigropalmatus)

This unusual frog glides from tree to tree
in the rainforest of Borneo using huge webbed
feet. Females make a wet foamy bubble
nest for their eggs.

SPRING PEEPER FROG (Pseudacris crucifer)

In the USA, male spring peepers
gather at breeding ponds
and call loudly to females.

SHARK

A shark can have as many as 3,000 teeth in rows one behind the other, so a shark is never without its bite. They have an excellent sense of smell, eyes that are better at seeing movement than ours, and they can sense the electricity in their prey's nerves. Sharks are as important in the marine world as big cats, hawks, and other predators are on land, and yet we kill more than 100 million of them every year!

SCALLOPED HAMMERHEAD SHARK ★
(Sphyrna lewini)

The strange head shape of this shark helps with all-around vision and swimming.

COOKIECUTTER SHARK (Isistius brasiliensis)

These little, cigar-shaped sharks take bites out of large sea creatures, leaving holes like a cookie cutter!

PORT JACKSON SHARK
(Heterodontus portusjacksoni)

This Australian shark eats sea urchins and shellfish, and lays corkscrew-shaped eggs.

BLUE SHARK ★ (Prionace glauca)

The blue shark is a fast-swimming fish eater.

500 SPECIES

GREAT WHITE SHARK ★
(Carcharodon carcharias)

This deadly predator is longer than a car, with teeth like steak knives. It hunts fish, seals, whales, and dolphins.

GOBLIN SHARK (Mitsukurina owstoni)

This strange shark lies in deep water and that's about all we know about it!

DWARF LANTERN SHARK (Etmopterus perryi)

The smallest shark, only found off the coasts of Venezuela and Colombia.

WHALE SHARK ★ (Rhincodon typus)
The biggest fish in the sea, the whale shark has tiny peg-like teeth for eating plankton.

BUTTERFLY

QUEEN ALEXANDRA'S BIRDWING BUTTERFLY ★ (*Ornithoptera alexandrae*)

The world's largest butterfly, found only in the rainforest in Papua New Guinea. Males are smaller and more brightly colored than females.

CLEOPATRA (*Gonepteryx Cleopatra*)

When they fold their wings, the undersides are green and look just like leaves.

Bright red spines warn predators that this caterpillar is poisonous.

COMMON POSTMAN (*Heliconius melpomene*)

Found in Central America and Brazil.

MENELAUS BLUE MORPHO BUTTERFLY (*Morpho menelaus*)

The bright blue on top of the wing says "Here I am" to other morphos, and the brown underneath lets these butterflies hide in rainforest shadows.

SONORAN BLUE (*Philotes sonorensis*)

These butterflies live in rocky outcrops and cliffs in deserts and feed on succulent plants.

Itchy hairs help keep predators away.

20,000 SPECIES

GIANT SWALLOWTAIL BUTTERFLY (Papilio cresphontes)
Birds peck the eye pattern on the tail streamers—allowing the butterfly to escape with just a pecked wing.

These caterpillars are camouflaged to look like bird poo.

ORANGE OAKLEAF
(Kallima inachus)

This butterfly can be different colors and sizes, depending on whether it hatches in the wet season or dry season.

MONARCH BUTTERFLY (Danaus plexippus)
Some butterflies can fly long distances. Monarchs fly from the northern USA to as far as Mexico.

Hanging from a twig, the chrysalis looks like a bit of a leaf.

Stripes warn predators that this caterpillar tastes horrible.

EUROPEAN PEACOCK (Aglais io)

The eye spots scare off predators. The chrysalis can be dark or light, to match the background.

As soon as they hatch, these caterpillars build a web nest to hide in.

Caterpillars are baby butterflies. The two animals look so different because of their very different lifestyles. All a caterpillar has to do is eat and grow, so it has a tube-like body, with a chewing mouth and legs to move it to the next meal. When it's grown enough, it makes a chrysalis and, inside, changes into an adult butterfly with eyes, antennae, and wings, and a mouth like a rolled-up straw for sipping sugary nectar from flowers.

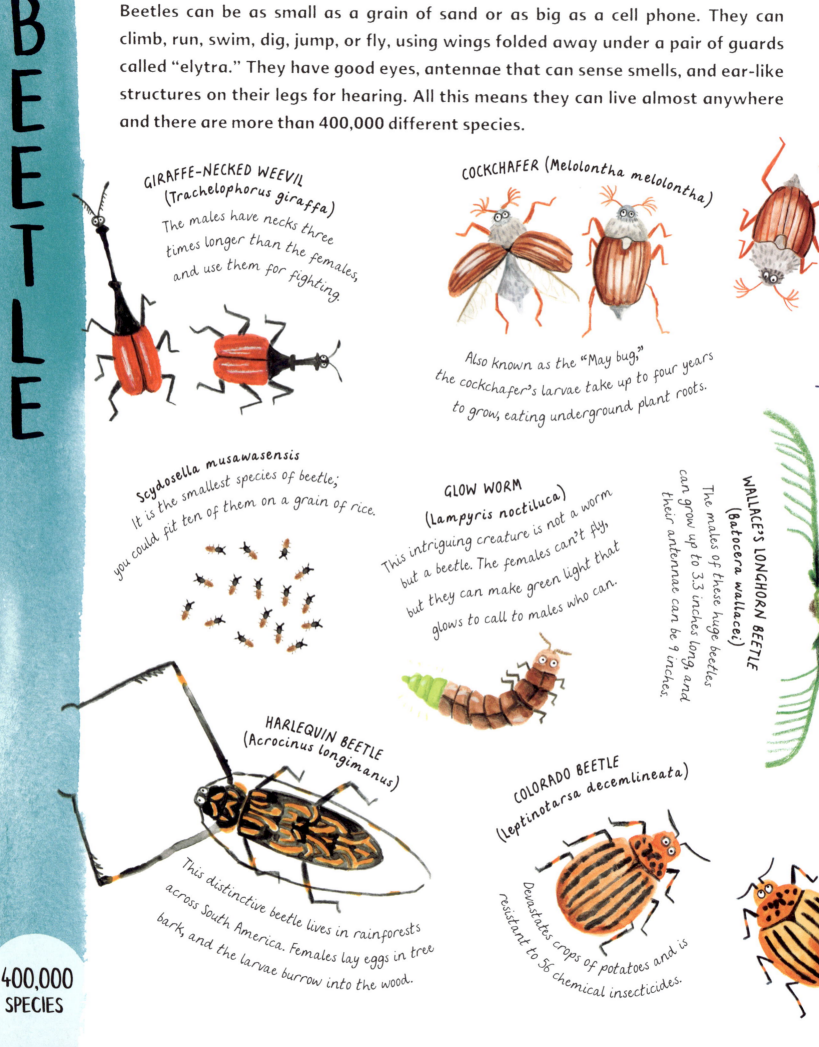

BEETLE

Beetles can be as small as a grain of sand or as big as a cell phone. They can climb, run, swim, dig, jump, or fly, using wings folded away under a pair of guards called "elytra." They have good eyes, antennae that can sense smells, and ear-like structures on their legs for hearing. All this means they can live almost anywhere and there are more than 400,000 different species.

GIRAFFE-NECKED WEEVIL (Trachelophorus giraffa)
The males have necks three times longer than the females, and use them for fighting.

COCKCHAFER (Melolontha melolontha)
Also known as the "May bug," the cockchafer's larvae take up to four years to grow, eating underground plant roots.

Scydosella musawasensis
It is the smallest species of beetle; you could fit ten of them on a grain of rice.

GLOW WORM (Lampyris noctiluca)
This intriguing creature is not a worm but a beetle. The females can't fly, but they can make green light that glows to call to males who can.

WALLACE'S LONGHORN BEETLE (Batocera wallacei)
The males of these huge beetles can grow up to 3.3 inches long, and their antennae can be 9 inches.

HARLEQUIN BEETLE (Acrocinus longimanus)
This distinctive beetle lives in rainforests across South America. Females lay eggs in tree bark, and the larvae burrow into the wood.

COLORADO BEETLE (Leptinotarsa decemlineata)
Devastates crops of potatoes and is resistant to 56 chemical insecticides.

400,000 SPECIES

GOLIATH BEETLE (Goliathus giganteus)

The goliath is the very largest beetle and lives on fruit and tree sap in the African forests.

This is a baby Goliath beetle. It lives underground and takes four months to grow big enough to turn into an adult.

FROG-LEGGED LEAF BEETLE (Sagra buqueti)
Males use their massive back legs for fighting over females, whose legs are normal size.

DEVIL'S COACH BEETLE (Ocypus olens)
Known for raising its abdomen and opening its jaws when threatened, this beetle also gives off a foul smell.

AFRICAN DUNG BEETLE (Scarabaeus zambesianus)

Rolls animal poo in a ball, buries it, and lays an egg on top so that the larva can feast when it hatches.

SEVEN-SPOT LADYBUG (Coccinella septempunctata)
Adults and their spiky larvae both eat aphids. One ladybug can eat up to 5,000 aphids in its year-long life.

BEE

LEAF-CUTTER BEE
(Megachile centuncularis)
The females of this species make tiny nests inside plant stems, for just one egg and larva.

COMMON CARDER BEE
(Bombus pascuorum)
Queen carder bees make nests of moss for their colonies of up to 150 workers.

ORANGE-TAILED MINING BEE
(Andrena haemorrhoa)
The females make burrows and fill each with pollen to feed their larvae.

RED-TAILED CUCKOO BUMBLEBEE
(Bombus rupestris)
The queens lay their eggs in the nests of other bumblebees, to be raised by another queen's workers.

AFRICAN GIANT CARPENTER BEE
(Xylocopa nigrita)
Carpenter bees make little holes in wood in which to lay their eggs.

ORCHID BEE (Euglossa cordata)
The males of this species visit flowers to collect their scents and then store them in pouches in their legs to attract females.

Most bees don't make honey. Some don't have a stinger. Not all make beeswax nests for their young, and many live on their own. But all sip nectar, feed their larvae on pollen, and carry pollen from flower to flower. Without this pollination, many plants—including fruits, nuts, and vegetables that we eat—could not make seeds and would die out. Bees are very, very important!

22,000 SPECIES

RED-TAILED BUMBLEBEE (Bombus lapidarius)
These bumblebees live in small nests with one queen and up to 200 workers.

STINGLESS BEES
(eg Melipona quadrifasciata)
Live in colonies like honeybees but each wax cell is filled with all the food the larvae will need from the start.

HONEYBEE (Apis mellifera)
The honeybee lives in colonies of 50,000 but just the queen lays eggs, which she deposits in wax cells. The worker bees feed the larvae as they grow.

CRAB

JAPANESE SPIDER CRAB
(Macrocheira kaempferi)

HORNED GHOST CRAB (Ocypode ceratophthalma)
Eyes on stalks help all crabs, like these beach scavengers, look out for food and danger.

ATLANTIC BLUE CRAB (Callinectes sapidus)
Crabs shells don't stretch, so the hard shells are shed as the crab grows. Underneath is a new, soft shell that takes a few days to harden.

Found in deep water around 1,968 feet. They have a leg span of 9.8 feet and can weigh as much as a 6-year-old child.

Crabs have their skeletons on the outside, and jointed legs like insects, but unlike insects, almost all crabs live in water, mostly in the sea. A few can survive on land, but all must return to water to lay their eggs. All crabs walk sideways on four pairs of legs; the fifth pair are pincers for grabbing food. Some crabs are predators, but others are scavengers and are natural recyclers of dead plants and animals.

FIDDLER CRAB (Uca perplexa)
Males signal to females from their burrows in the mud by waving one big, bright claw.

SAND BUBBLER CRAB (Scopimera globosa)
At low tide thousands of sand bubbler crabs eat tiny plants and animals caught in the sands on tropical beaches.

COCONUT CRAB (Birgus latro)
Can grow so large that their massive claws can slice through coconut shells on the Pacific and Indian Ocean beaches where they live.

COMMON SHORE CRAB (Carcinus maenas)
Lives in cool coastal waters worldwide, grabs prey such as shellfish and worms with its claws.

COMMON HERMIT CRAB (Pagurus bernhardus)
Hermit crabs are really lobsters without a strong shell and use the empty shells of mollusks instead.

SLUG

COMMON KEELED SLUG (Tandonia budapestensis)

Many land slugs, like this species, live underground eating plant roots and seeds.

LEAF SHEEP (Costasiella kuroshimae)
Just 0.2 inches long, this sea slug grazes on tiny plants.

LEOPARD SLUG (Limax maximus)

Typically for land slugs this is a recycler, eating dead plants and animals, including other slugs.

CRESTED NEMBROTHA (Nembrotha cristata)
like many sea slugs, its bright color warns that this slug can sting!

SEA BUNNY (Jorunna parva)

LETTUCE SEA SLUG (Elysia crispata)
Its green color comes from tiny plants living in the slug's body.

Their "ears" are just feelers that sense tastes in the water.

Slugs are really just snails, but without the shell. Their soft bodies dry out easily, so they hide under stones and in the soil and come out at night. They slide around on slime made by their skin and have a spiny tongue to scrape at food. Sea slugs are their more colorful cousins.

60,000+ SPECIES

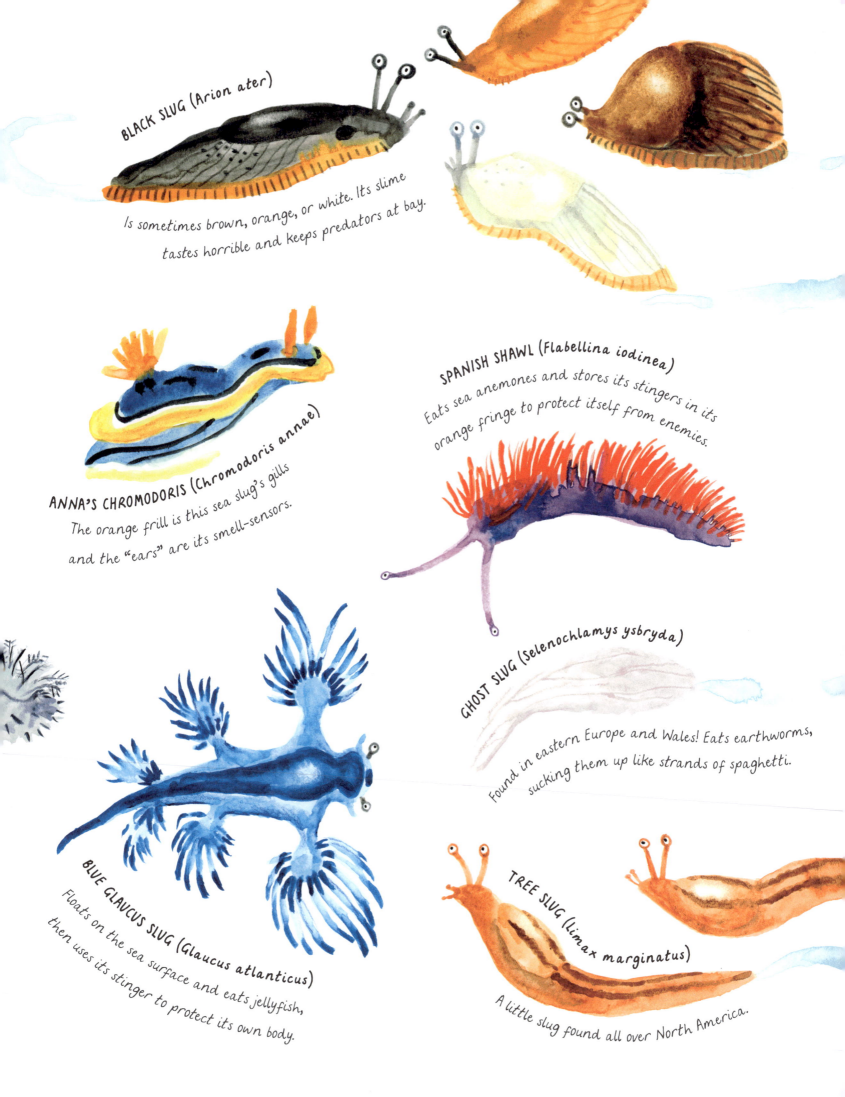

BLACK SLUG (Arion ater)

Is sometimes brown, orange, or white. Its slime tastes horrible and keeps predators at bay.

SPANISH SHAWL (Flabellina iodinea)

Eats sea anemones and stores its stingers in its orange fringe to protect itself from enemies.

ANNA'S CHROMODORIS (Chromodoris annae)

The orange frill is this sea slug's gills and the "ears" are its smell-sensors.

GHOST SLUG (Selenochlamys ysbryda)

Found in eastern Europe and Wales! Eats earthworms, sucking them up like strands of spaghetti.

BLUE GLAUCUS SLUG (Glaucus atlanticus)

Floats on the sea surface and eats jellyfish, then uses its stinger to protect its own body.

TREE SLUG (Limax marginatus)

A little slug found all over North America.

GRASS

AFRICAN ELEPHANT GRASS
(Pennisetum purpureum)

"Elephant grass" is a single name for three different species of tropical grass that can grow to 9.8 feet tall in a year.

OATS (Avena sativa)
Oats can be grown where it is too cold and wet for wheat or barley.

EURASIAN ELEPHANT GRASS
(Saccharum ravennae)

SOUTH ASIAN ELEPHANT GRASS
(Miscanthus fuscus)

ANTARCTIC HAIR GRASS
(Deschampsia antarctica)

This species is one of the very few plants that can survive the deep cold of the Antarctic.

WHEAT (Triticum spp)
There are many species of wheat that can grow in hot climates. Durum wheat (Triticum durum) grows well in dry places.

Grasses are plants with long skinny leaves that can grow even where there is very little rain or soil. Their feathery plumes are flowers, and these are pollinated by the wind. Unlike other plants, grasses grow from the bottom not the top, so when their tips are eaten by animals, they keep on growing. Many animals depend on grasses for food, and they feed us, too; all our most important crops are grasses, even if they don't have the word "grass" in their name.

12,000 SPECIES

BLUE GRAMA GRASS (Bouteloua gracilis)
Growing in the North American prairies, this grass once fed the vast herds of bison.

TOM THUMB GRASS (Dregeochloa pumila)
Possibly the world's smallest grass and the only one that can store water in its leaves.

BARLEY (Hordeum vulgare)
One of the crops grown by the first farmers 10,000 years ago.

ASIAN RICE (Oryza sativa)
Grown in flooded fields in hot countries, rice feeds more people than any other single crop.

MAIZE (Zea mays)
First grown in Mexico 4,000 years ago, there are many different varieties grown for different purposes.

DRAGON BAMBOO (Dendrocalamus giganteus)
All 1,400 species of bamboos are types of grass. The biggest grow to a forest size: 81-96 feet tall.

T R E E

ENGLISH OAK
(Quercus robur)

Found in the UK and Europe, the oak can live for 1,000 years and make a home for more than 300 different kinds of animals and plants.

COCONUT PALM (Cocos nucifera)

The coconut, native to the islands of the Pacific and Indian Oceans, is just one of 2,600 different species of palm tree, which only grow where there are no frosts.

GREAT BASIN BRISTLECONE PINE
(Pinus longaeva)

These ancient trees from the western USA can grow in cold, dry, rocky places where no other tree survives. Some individuals are over 4,000 years old, making them the oldest living things on earth.

GINGKO ★ (Gingko biloba)
Fossils show that this Chinese species, also known as the "maidenhair tree," has been around for 270 million years.

A tree is any plant with a strong, woody stem or trunk supporting a crown of leaves. There are about three trillion individual trees on earth, which together make forests that help to create clean air and rain water. Each species of tree can be home for hundreds of different species of animals and smaller plants. Tropical forests, where thousands of species of tree grow, are packed with life.

100,000 SPECIES

DAHURIAN LARCH
(*Larix gmelinii*)

This hardy larch, with tough needle-like leaves, grows farther north than any other tree, appearing hundreds of miles inside the Arctic Circle, where winter temperatures can drop to -94°F.

GIANT SEQUOIA OR REDWOOD ★
(*Sequoiadendron giganteum*)

These giant trees from Northern California are not quite the tallest trees on earth, but they are the heaviest; their trunks are up to 55 feet across—wide enough to park a truck inside.

LIGHT RED MERANTI TREE ★
(*Shorea johorensis*)

Light red meranti trees are one of 500 different species of huge rainforest trees called dipterocarps. They grow all over the tropics, but the greatest variety is in Borneo.

KAPOK TREE (*Ceiba pentandra*)

The kapok, found in South America and West Africa, is the tallest tree in the forests where it grows.

CHINESE MAGNOLIA ★ (*Magnolia sinensis*)

Only fifty of these beautiful flowering trees are left in their home of Central China.

MUSHROOM

Not all living things are plants or animals. Mushrooms belong to a third important group: fungi. They are nature's recyclers, breaking down dead bodies and poo into nutrients that can be reused by living things. They are in the soil, in water and inside trees. We don't see them until they make "fruiting bodies"—the mushrooms and toadstools whose job is to make the dust-like "seeds" of fungi, called spores.

LILAC PINKGILL (Entoloma porphyrophaeum)
Found in grasslands in Europe and Asia, the fruiting bodies of this species can last for weeks before being eaten by slugs.

COLLARED EARTHSTAR (Geastrum triplex)
The "rays" of the earthstar fold and unfold in damp weather to release spores.

VIOLET CORAL (Clavaria zollingeri)
The main part is its hyphae: fine threads under soil or inside plants. Only the fruiting bodies are brightly colored.

FLY AGARIC (Amanita muscaria)
This distinctive toadstool, found all over the world, lives around the roots of forest trees. Its brightly colored fruiting body contains poisons.

HORSE MUSHROOM (Agaricus arvensis)
Found worldwide in fields and grasslands, the fruiting bodies appear in late summer and autumn after rainfall.

75,000+ SPECIES

MYCENA (Mycena chlorophos)

This tiny mushroom grows on tropical forest trees and glows with pale green light in the dark.

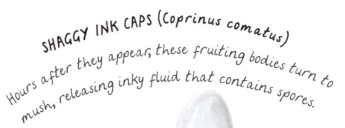

SHAGGY INK CAPS (Coprinus comatus)

Hours after they appear, these fruiting bodies turn to mush, releasing inky fluid that contains spores.

WITCHES' BUTTER (Tremella mesenterica)

This wood-eating species prefers recently fallen branches or dead ones that are still attached to the tree.

ARTIST'S BRACKET (Ganoderma applanatum)

This species can kill a whole tree by eating the live wood. Its big, hard fruiting bodies stick out from trunks and branches like ledges.

WOOD EAR (Auricularia auricula-judae)

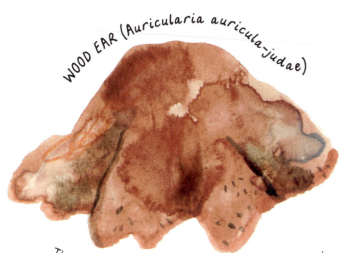

The hyphae of this widespread fungus grow inside trees eating dead wood.

AMPHIBIAN

Amphibians have thin, wet skin, through which they can breathe on land and in water. It must stay moist for them to survive. They lay eggs, usually in fresh water, which hatch into legless "tadpoles." They breathe through gills, before growing legs, losing their gills, and changing into adult form.

BALEEN

These are the long, narrow plates that fill the mouths of baleen whales, such as blue whales, humpbacks, fins, and minkes. They are made of the same material as your fingernails, and have bristly edges that overlap, creating a sieve that separates krill and small fish from seawater.

BIRD

Birds breathe air, have feathers, and are warm-blooded. They have two legs and two wings, which are usually used for flight or, in some species such as penguins, for swimming, and occasionally for neither, as is the case for ostriches. All birds lay hard-shelled eggs. Over 9,800 species are known.

BREEDING

Breeding is the process by which animals mate, have babies, and care for them to help them survive.

CAMOUFLAGE

This is when an animal matches its environment in order to stay hidden and avoid being eaten, or in order to sneak up on its prey without being seen!

CRUSTACEAN

Crustaceans' bodies have a hard, shell-like exoskeleton, five pairs of jointed legs, and two pairs of antennae. Most live in the sea or freshwater but there are a few, such as woodlice, that live in moist environments on land. Over 67,000 species are known.

FISH

Fish have no legs and breathe underwater through gills. They live their whole lives in fresh or seawater. Most lay eggs, which must stay in water to hatch. In a few species, females hatch eggs inside their body and give birth to live young. Over 30,000 species are known.

FUNGUS

Fungi (the plural of fungus) live by digesting dead material. They can be microscopic, like the yeast that makes bread rise, or large, such as the fungi that break down dead trees. They are vital recyclers, and animals and plants could not live without them. Over 75,000 species of fungus are known.

HIBERNATION

Creatures that sleep through the winter to avoid the cold and lack of food go into hibernation. They eat nothing and live off their body fat, slowing their breathing and heartbeat down so they don't run out of energy before spring comes!

INSECT

Insects' bodies are covered in a tough, armor-like exoskeleton. They have three pairs of jointed legs and a body divided into head, thorax, and abdomen. They usually have two pairs of wings. Over 900,000 species are known.

INVERTEBRATES

Invertebrates don't have a backbone or internal skeleton, but many of them, such as insects and crustaceans, have a tough exoskeleton to give their bodies shape and protection, or, in the cases of mollusks, a shell.

GLOSSARY

MAMMAL
Mammals breathe air, are warm-blooded (which means they can keep their bodies at a steady temperature), and have fur. Females give birth to live young (except for the spiny anteaters and the duck-billed platypus, which lay eggs) and feed their babies on their own milk. Over 4,600 species of mammal are known (including humans).

METAMORPHOSIS
The process by which an animal changes its body form into something that is different, for example, tadpoles into frogs, and caterpillars into butterflies. Metamorphosis is very common among invertebrates.

MOLLUSK
Mollusks have soft bodies, often with one or two shells for protection and a tooth-covered tongue, called a "radula," for scraping or biting food. They have no legs, although some, such as squid and octopus, have tentacles but no shell. Most live in the sea but a few, such as snails and slugs, can survive on land. Over 100,000 species are known.

NOCTURNAL
An animal that is active at night and sleeps by day is nocturnal.

PLANT
A plant is a living thing that can make its own food from sunlight, air, and water. Some plants are too tiny for us to see, and some are the biggest living things on earth. Grass, trees, seaweed, flowers, and microscopic diatoms are all plants. Over 400,000 different species are known—but that's not counting the microscopic ones.

POLLINATION

In pollination, the male parts of a plant, called "anthers," make dust-like pollen that travels to the female parts, called "stigma," to fertilize its seeds, so they can grow into new plants. In some plants, such as grasses, pollen is carried by the wind. In others, the flower is colored and filled with sweet nectar to attract insects, birds, or mammals, which carry pollen from one flower to another.

PREDATOR

An animal that lives by hunting, killing, and eating other animals—its "prey"—is called a predator.

REPTILE

Reptiles breathe air, have a tough scaly skin, and are cold-blooded (which means they can't keep warmer or cooler than their environment). Most lay leathery eggs, but some hatch their eggs inside their bodies and give birth to live young. Over 7,700 species are known.

SPECIES (pronounced SPEE-SEES or SPEE-SHEES)

A species is a kind of living thing. Each species has features that help it to survive and make it different from every other species, for example, long ears to hear predators or spines to protect leaves. Living things can usually only breed with other members of their own species. Scientists have named and described almost two million different species so far, but there could be as many as 10 million or more!

VERTEBRATES

Mammals, birds, reptiles, amphibians, and fish are all vertebrates, meaning they have a hard vertebral column or backbone, which is part of their internal skeleton. This supports and protects the soft parts of their body, giving them shape and helping them to move.

TREE OF LIFE

The story of life on Earth is like a tree. It began growing around 3.8 billion years ago with single-celled living things too tiny to see. Since then it has grown and branched out, as more and bigger forms of life evolved over millions of years. All the living things alive today are the twigs. You can trace each twig back to see the branch and the trunk from which it came.

Spiders

Insects

Crabs and lobsters

Segmented worms

Snails, slugs, octopuses

Sea urchins and starfish

Flatworms

INVERTEBRATES

Jellyfish, corals, and anemones

Sponges

ANIMALS

SIMPLE SINGLE-CELLED LIFE/BACTERIA

FIRST
SINGLE-
CELLED LIFE

Mammals

Birds

Reptiles and amphibians

Fish

VERTEBRATES

Clubmosses

Horsetails

Ferns

Lichens

Hornworts

Firs and pines

Plants with flowers

Mosses

PLANTS

FUNGI

COMPLEX SINGLE-CELLED LIFE